All Scripture references taken from the KJV of the Holy Bible, unless otherwise indicated.

<u>Astral Projected Spirit Spouse, DIE!</u>

Dr. Marlene Miles

Freshwater Press 2024

ISBN: 978-1-963164-22-0

eBook Version

Table of Contents

**I am often astounded
at my own ignorance.**

Astral Projected

Spirit Spouse,

DIE

Freshwater

Introduction

After finding out what a spirit spouse is a few years ago, I also found out that there are more than 30 different types of spirit spouses. The only thing worse than finding that out is to become aware that you have one, or worse—more than one. Or the worst--, you're somehow *okay* with it?

Lord, forbid.

The Word says that God's people perish for a lack of knowledge, so the research began. Since this research is not all in one place, the Spirit of the Lord has impressed upon me to record my findings for you and for posterity.

This book will include information on the spirit spouse that astral projects into the life of its victim(s) and how to fight this.

The Astral World

The astral world is the spirit world. It is the world that is unseen by most but can be seen by some who are gifted to see it, or those who have chosen to see it. Some are gifted by God to see it, but they are too afraid to do so. I pray, by the Grace and Mercy of God if you are gifted by God to be a seer, that you will be a seer for the Kingdom of God and never be tricked or hijacked into using your gift for any other reason, purpose, or kingdom, in the Name of Jesus.

I bind and paralyze the *spirit of fear* off of you, your life for the sake of the Kingdom of God. You have a purpose in Earth; your gifts were given for purpose. Let the Love of God and the power of His might bring you to your purpose and protect, teach, strengthen, and keep you. Amen.

The astral plane (world) is a nonphysical level or realm of being, separate from the physical one accessible from it by means of one's *astral body*. To see this realm does not mean that you have to go there. It is believed to be inhabited by angels and other nonphysical beings, such as lost souls; sounds like Purgatory to me. Those who use psychic powers may be those who have been gifted of God, but have misused or abused their gifts, and been hijacked for use by the kingdom of darkness.

Trauma, which the devil loves, can thrust a person into a dissociative state where their body is present, but not their soul. A person automatically may do this to cope with the ordeal at hand. Where does that soul go at that time? Into the astral? Humans are very vulnerable out there.

The astral holds demons, disembodied entities--, lost souls, demons, devils, spiritual wickedness in high places. High places on Earth they are the wicked altars that burn on mountain sides in witchcraft-riddled cultures. High places where all that wickedness is, IS the astral plane the 2nd Heaven. Evil altar workers invoke devils from the 2nd Heaven to bring them to Earth to do evil; that's what evil altars are for (Ephesians 6:12). Why would you *go* there, purposefully?

For serving the wrong kingdom, those people will see hell. For not using your God-given gift at all, there will be repercussions.

Astral Projection

Translation is a God-led, God-inspired or God-called out-of-body experience.

In 2 Corinthians 12:2, Paul says regarding the astral planes:

I know a man in Christ who fourteen years ago was caught up to the third heaven. Whether it was in the body or out of the body I do not know—God knows.

Apostle John, while on the island of Patmos, wrote the Book of the Revelation. He saw visions of Heaven and recorded them. If John was *in* Heaven, he was **translated** there by God; John did not take it upon himself to roam about the universe and *accidentally* end up in Heaven.

To be absent from the body means that one should be present with the Lord. That means not anywhere else, but with the Lord. If your spirit man is built up you will have the power to resist evil calls or evil summons into the astral or to other horrible places. If your spirit man is weak and unfed, you will be as a puppet.

If you are called out of your body by the devil, any dark powers, or an evil human agent, you'd be well advised not to go. However, when you are sleeping you may not be aware of being called into the astral, and you may not have resistance to the power behind the *who* or the *what* is calling.

When astral projection is self-willed, that is self-led, which is what yogis and other "spiritualists" are teaching on the internet, that is occultic mysticism; it is demonically led.

Ever how you get in the astral plane, if it is not of God and God-sponsored, it is perilous. It is perilous to try to go there by yourself, it is perilous *while* you're there, and it is perilous when trying to return. If you want to collect demons, then go on out there. But know that the demons you collect are not anything that you can control. People think that demons are floating about with nothing to do, like genies and if they can capture one or speak to one that they will have "powers" at their command. This is not so. There are no demons that you can control **in and of yourself.** If a demon is being "controlled" it is because it wants you to think that you are in control of it – for a time.

By the power of God, and by the Word of God and His Angelic Hosts you can command demons to do the will of God. Else, those demons will run all over you and your life. When that happens, things will run amok, you will be not just inconvenienced, but very uncomfortable. They will torment and terrorize you, since they come to steal, kill and destroy. To solve this, you will need deliverance from these entities.

So, are you playing around with astral projecting? Self-led astral projecting is the perfect way to collect demons that come to steal, kill, and destroy you and your life, even though your own motives may be to use them to destroy someone else's life.

Perhaps you're a *victim* of astral projection and don't yet realize it. The following are some dream signs that astral projection is happening in your life:

You see strange faces in the dream. Disembodied *spirits* will put on masquerade faces. Some of these faces aren't even faces, real faces, whole faces or believable faces.

You see yourself flying in the dream. Since these *spirits* have met you out there unescorted in the astral plane, you are now summonable. You've been summoned somewhere to do something. Believe this, if a demon has summoned you to a place, it's not a good place. It might be a satanic circle, a coven, a graveyard, and evil forest, under the waters, or worse.

Experiencing a strange loss of money and properties is another way they announce their arrival and evil works in your life. Think of demons as opportunists. If you're floating about in the astral plane, out there on your own and they know it, they can to do pretty much anything to you. Stealing is the first thing. You'd better repent to God and pray: *spirit of loss* in my life be bound and paralyzed, in the Name of Jesus.

Seeing yourself as a witch in the dream means you've been summoned somewhere, probably to a witch's coven. You may have been summoned for a witch's court and put on trial. There are also evil councils that a human can be called to. You may never know where you go or where you've been when summoned unless the Holy Spirit brings it back to your remembrance and reveals it to you. If you're courageous enough, when you wake up in the morning, ask the Holy Spirit,

- *Where did I go in my sleep? Where was I?*
- *What did I do?*
- *Who was I with? Even ask,*
- *How did I get there?*

Lights going off or on in some area of a home is a sure sign of a demonic presence. Of course, in the natural, check your electrical wiring for your safety.

Seeing a shadow or figure in the mirror, when it should just be you--, that's a *monitoring spirit.*

In your waking life, seeing people who you **know** are dead as alive. Isn't that torment?

Seeing evil *spirits* in the home. These are UNCLEAN SPIRITS – CAST them out!

Seeing your mother dressed as a witch is another sign. As well, seeing yourself in a forest, river, or at altars, Seeing yourself swimming in dreams, especially in dirty water.

In the natural, when you wake up to cuts, scrapes, or scratches on your body that many times is astral projection attacks in the night while you are asleep.

With astral projection some of what happens is you going places and some of it is stuff coming *to* you. Either way, you've lost control because your human power, on your own is not greater than what is out there. Seriously, logically how do you plan to corale or control anything that is stronger than you? Demons are not horses or animals that you can train; **you either take dominion over them, or they will take dominion over you.**

The only way to command authority over demons is if you come in the Name of the Lord. If you come with the anointing and authority of the Lord. If you come in the power of the Lord in the Company of the Lord, or with His Heavenly Host and Angelic Warriors. Warning: You can not cavort with these demons and then expect to command or control them. That's another reason why you don't go out into the astral willfully and on your own, playing around with what you should be exercising dominion over. Dominion is only possible in Christ.

- Every astral projection assigned against me, die by Fire, die by Fire, die by Fire, die by Fire, die by Fire, in Jesus' Name.

Coming to You

An astral traveler can project into your space, your room, your life. It is said that a person's astral body, also called a *body of light,* can separate from the physical body and soul travel or travel into different planes of existence.

Witches, warlocks, wizards, shamans, yogis, and swamis are said to astral project. I have heard stories of men, who look like regular people--, professionals even--, being rejected by women, and then telling the woman who rejected him, *Don't worry, I'll see you tonight.* And surely enough there have been many reports of women being assaulted in their beds at night – not just in dreams, this is more than a dream, this is worse than a dream, this is more real than just a dream. This is an astral projected someone or some*thing* coming for the sexual rights of that woman that he or she couldn't get in the waking life.

The wicked traveler doesn't always manifest as a human, it can come as an animal or a beast. This is why, when someone says they had a dream of having sex with a dog or other animal, these heinous dreams need to be prayer treated as they are not just dreams. This *thing* that was seeking revenge for being rejected and came as a man or a beast and took what it wanted all along.

Well, it comes to take what it *thinks* it wants. It *thinks* it wants sex, but sex, forced or not, takes far more away from a person than one might think. The person attacking the other is not taking the virtues, the devil is stealing the virtues. That indicates that the evil human is only selfishly going for the obvious. While both of them are distracted the virtues are being drained off by a more powerful force or entity. These devil transactions are sometimes very complicated. The attacker may be rewarded for doing evil, but the devil is the handler, he will get far more out of this than either of the humans. Plus, he will own one or both of them now to do more of his evil bidding.

If it is having sex with the person, it is as a *spirit spouse*. The astral projecting spirit spouse is a human spirit, or *of* a human spirit and has to be handled a certain way.

Projected spirit spouse – witch doctors, voodoo priests, occultists, et cetera can use astral projection to have spiritual sex with a victim.

A spirit spouse is foul, evil, defiling, not of God, and it must DIE, in the Name of Jesus. It comes to defile, and once defiled you can be robbed of almost anything you have. You could also be terrorized by **people** who astral project into your life, into your room, into your dreams who come as spirit spouses. You can be tormented and terrorized by astral travelers, witches, and warlocks who will use masquerade to trick you or have you thinking someone *other than a demon* is "visiting" you or talking with you, in or out of the dream. But, they come to steal, kill and destroy—to fight you, stop you, derail you, to take your life off track, your marriage off track, and/or take your health off the rails.

They will have you thinking it's your dear lost loved one, it's Elvis Pressly or some other celebrity you admire. **IT. IS. A. DEMON.**

How can a person be a victim of such? If you're unsaved, it's easy to be a spiritual victim of any kind—including astral rape.

If you are saved and prayerless, careless, sinning, unrepentant, or ignorant of the devil's devices, it can still happen. Saved, or unsaved, if you need deliverance because you are packed with demons who cling onto you any way they can, you can be a victim again and again. One way they cling onto you is by astral projection and other sins that you may commit yourself. These demons open the door for you to be victimized. You need deliverance. What is *in* you could have always been there from your birth. It could be a family, generational, or ancestral curse. You could have been dedicated to the dark kingdom by any person, usually someone related to you by blood, possibly known to you, but the dedication could be unknown to you.

You could have dedicated your own child and not even realize it. It could be as simple as someone saying when they are a teenager that they would give their first born for _____ whatever they felt they desperately wanted at that moment. Ten years go by; the person is now 27, married with their first child on the way. They do not remember that they were so hungry for a pizza 10 years ago and that they said something hyperbolic, so ridiculous, and everyone in the room, laughed like it was a joke, **but the devil heard it.**

Your first born is now dedicated to Satan and you have no knowledge that it happened or when it happened. There are other sinister ways this could happen as well.

People who are known to say anything, especially in desperate situations, are some of the most dangerous people in the world. If you are related to them or associate with them, your wellbeing and life may be in peril. No, I don't need to be around people with colorful speech like that. This is why the Word says not to jest. You could say something, just be kidding and never renounce what you said, but only in your mind know, *I was just kidding.* Well, you never countered what you said --, so you gave your first born for a pizza.

*Did you even **get** the pizza?*

Astral projection (astral travel) is is thought to have occurred since ancient times and happens worldwide in many cultures. It is demonic but people don't tell you that. It is mostly an occultic practice.

It is packaged as New Age, but there is nothing new about New Ageism, it is occultic, pagan, and demonic practices. Folks believe they've taken the "power" from such practices but left all the "bad" stuff. This is not possible, just as *wet* comes with water.

Ancient Egyptians believed in astral travel. Amazon and other tribes soul travel to consult celestial beings for healing. They go to the moon, or to the *brother* of the moon to get the name of a newborn baby. They believed to travel to the mountain to ask for hunting success to feed their families. Or they believe they travel deep into the river to get help from other *beings* down there--, marine kingdom, folks!

Innuits think similarly. The sad thing about this is all the places they go to ask for, and all the things they ask for the devil <u>can</u> supply all of that stuff. The devil can ***misname*** your child. The devil can heal – usually by shifting the sickness somewhere else in the body for a while, or to someone else completely. The devil can provide game for the hunter, and sandwiches, and pizzas in modern times. But there is a price to pay for anything the devil does for you.

Famously, humans say be careful what you ask for. Yeah, that's true and be careful *who* you're asking. If you are asking for something ungodly, automatically that request will go to the second heaven, where the throne of Satan is. Even if you're asking for something Godly, or innocently but asking or seeking the wrong way, you may roll up on the psychic and second heaven answer and mistakenly take it. We must learn God, talk to God and approach God properly.

East Indian cultures take astral projection to a whole other level. Yogis and Swami's, who live in a polytheistic (idolatrous) culture astral travel all the time and they believe they are using it for "good." They also believe that those who do this are spiritually advanced. Perhaps they are, but advanced by what *spirit*?

The devil.

In Japanese culture it is believed that a person's soul can leave their body to appear before the object of their hatred to curse them or hurt them in some other way. This is similar to *evil eye*. Japan may be 1% Christian; they worship anything and everything, but will quickly tell you that they worship nothing. In China, Taoists believe similarly. So, should astral travel become anything you want to do of your own accord or have someone coach you into it? Of course not; non-Christians use it and celebrate it so Christians should not.

If you believe you can take astral travel out of Eastern mysticism and leave all the demons behind, that is the same as believing you can take the good or the power out of something and leave all the bad. It is not possible in spiritual matters. Demons come with the devil.

The Silver Cord

Christians believe there is a silver cord –

Yes, remember your Creator now while you
are young, before the silver cord of life snaps
and the golden bowl is broken. Don't wait
until the water jar is smashed at the spring
and the pulley is broken at the well.
(Ecclesiastes 12:6 NLT)

The silver cord, it is said, spiritually
tethers a man to his body so he can get back in to
his physical body once he has soul traveled.

Saints of God, Dear Readers, I'll tell you
what I personally know of a silver cord.

Years ago, I was in rehabilitation from a
debilitating car accident. In my late 20's. I was
beginning to bow over—my head was hanging
down. This was significant because I always had
been complimented on my great posture all my
life. There was so much pain in the neck and
shoulder area that I was beginning to bow over. I
had been in physical therapy, but nothing had

helped. I prayed and prayed. Months and even a year or more went by and I was still incapacitated. I sought God fervently and prayed. One day I was seated on my bed, praying, and I felt as though a silver cord was pulled up toward Heaven and lengthened and suddenly my posture, after all those months and months was made straight again as God intended and from my birth. I had a healthy spine; I had no more pain.

At that time, I knew nothing about a silver cord, but that is what I saw in the spirit as my back and spine were being straightened. I was healed. Praise God; the Lord is the lifter of my head. Amen.

But thou, O LORD, art a shield for me; my glory, and the lifter up of mine head. I cried unto the LORD with my voice, and he heard me out of his holy hill. Selah. I laid me down and slept; I awaked; for the LORD sustained me. (Psalm 3:3-5)

It's 1997. David Bryan, a legit Christian minister, and intercessor had adopted one of the daughters of Anton LaVey, the founder of the Church of Satan. One night, in the middle of serious spiritual warfare, Brian heard the Lord say, ***Cut LaVey's silver cord.***

In that heated warfare LaVey *bounced*, that means he couldn't get back into his own body after astral projecting because **his silver cord was cut**. There is only a certain amount of time that a person can be out of body before they are permanently locked out. But if their silver cord is cut, it is lights out to that astral traveler, and that means they become DEAD.

Satanists were praying to Satan. They were calling on Satan to help LaVey get back into his human body once they realized he was in trouble because of the warfare that the Christians, led by David Bryan had begun. LaVey had left his body to astral project to go and kill or destroy someone's life--, namely David Bryan whom he had threatened because Bryian was not returning LaVey's adult daughter to him, the astral projection victim. LaVey was coming at Brian through his own daughter, stating that he had a *birthright* to DJ LaVey.

But DJ had been saved, set free, delivered, and adopted by Bryan so LaVey no longer had birthright rights to this daughter, DJ.

After Anton LaVey died, Leviathan, LaVey's "power spirit" manifested in another of

LaVey's daughters. A female voice spoke through DJ and said, *"I hate you, you killed my father."*

Bryan asked, *"Who are you?"* It was another of Lavey's daughters who were still serving Satan projected into her sister. Bryan said, *"We have a right from Jesus Christ to cut his silver cord and we will do it to you also, if you don't go away."*

The voice said, *"I will go,"* and left immediately.

Thou shalt not tempt the Lord thy God, (Matthew 4:7). If willfully separating your soul or spirit from your body to go into the astral is **at the risk of death**, what game is this astral traveler playing? Isn't that tempting God, as if saying, Lord I'm about to do something really dangerous – keep me alive?

The wages of sin is death (Romans 6:23), can we not deduce that astral travel is sin? If there is the risk of death and a person chooses to do this, is this a form of suicide roulette--, quickly or slowly. Demons come to kill--, it may take a while, but that is what they come for.

Come Up Here

The astral plane is said to be inhabited by angels, demons, and *spirits*. Some say they visit different **times** and/or places; whatever this "world" is, surely was not built for humans, else we would all know about it and have ease in traveling there and returning. **God gave man Earth.**

The heaven, even the heavens, are the LORD'S: but the earth hath he given to the children of men. (Psalms 115:16)

God, by His Spirit, transcends all space and time. But we all know that when we pray and say we are going up to the high places to do warfare, we really don't believe that our soul has left our body. As we pray, our words are doing the work. Our words become *Spirit and Life* and they do certain work, spiritually speaking. Just as God's Word does not return to Him void, but it performs where and what He sends it to so will the Word perform when we speak it. That is why we pray the Word. We are not detaching our souls from our body, we are simply engaging in prayer.

God can *translate* us, however. If leaving the body is God-initiated and God-orchestrated you will go or be sent with protection. You hear person after person who give testimony that they went to Heaven, *or* hell and they were shown this that or the other. In all those testimonies, Jesus or an angel of the Lord is with them. They have angelic or spiritual **ESCORT**. They are not just thrust out into the astral plane to do as they please.

To be absent from the body is to be present with the Lord (2 Corinthians 5:8).

Present with the Lord means either in a Godly *translation* experience, or dead and in Glory.

Come up here...

And they heard a great voice from heaven saying unto them, Come up hither. And they ascended up to heaven in a cloud; and their enemies beheld them, (Revelations 11:12).

Folks can be called by the voice and the Word of God. With that anointing you are not on your own, but being *called* or *sent* with a Godly anointing is always safe and protected.

Self-willed astral travel or demonically charged astral travel, are both dangerous and can be deadly. There is no good to take out of it, leaving the bad stuff. If you are doing it by your own will, it is devil powered and if you believe you did it and are safe today, you are being *groomed* for something sinister. It's a set up.

The soul is not supposed to detach from the human body and go into the astral as if a person is tired of class and going for recess.

Shamans dance themselves into a trance and *dissociate*. A lot of tribes all over the world who use drums and drumbeats enter trances for similar reasons. Astral projection has been practiced for centuries as we have outlined.

Mistakenly, people, even a lot of Christians believe now that you can just do this. Yogis and mystics are teaching astral projection also called OBE, out of body experience, all over the internet. That does not make it of God; saints, do not do this. How do you know that once you indicate that you want to astral project that you are not signing up for some demonic *service*?

Yeah, you may go out a couple of times and everything seems fine, but now you've been initiated to astral travel and how do you know that you are not being called out to do things that you normally wouldn't do in the spirit, normally couldn't do, and those assignments are evil? How do you know?

The reason I mention this in this way is because **how do you know that you aren't the one initiating spirit sex?** I know of three separate women who when they asked the Lord to really show them what was going on with spirit spouse, they saw themselves in a relationship with some male and when he said he had to go, the two of the three women clung to this dream male. Yeah, the spirit spouse. This had been going on for so long, or they were so comfortable with it that they favored the spirit spouse but didn't know anything about it until they sought deliverance and asked the Lord to reveal the truth to them.

How in your dreams you are in different locations when this is happening? How do *you* know that **you** aren't the one captive to the dark side, who is enslaved to be a spirit spouse? If you are a spiritual captive, you must do what your jailer says. The real reason I'm mentioning this is that in a dream I asked someone, *Who do you think I am, your spirit spouse?*

How do you know that when you said you wanted to be an astral traveler that you didn't sign up for some evil service that the devil or his evil human agent use for their own benefit, or against other humans, and your spirit man just does what it is told in the dream?

- *Lord, deliver me from the sleep affliction of waking up so tired every morning, in the Name of Jesus. Where have I been? What have I been doing that I am tired after proper hours of sleep?*
- Lord, break me free from anything evil that I have knowingly or unknowingly signed up for or have been initiated into, in the Name of Jesus.
- Lord, if I am a blind witch or warlock, or I repent, renounce, and denounce all evil vows and alliances. Please deliver me today, in the Name of Jesus.

Sure, there are multiple kinds of spirit spouses, but the devil could confound a human by using another willing, evil or *compromised* human instead so the victim might have a hard time breaking free, or that they never break free. Can the devil use a human that doesn't know he or she is being used?

Do not owe the devil anything because that is as good as owing the devil everything. When you owe the devil, you owe everything, and it is generational. Do not do this to your family.

Christians do not astral project despite erroneous teachings in some so-called churches. This is a lie from the pit of hell. It's a deception from the realm of darkness. This is not a Christian practice. Christians may have what we would call out of body experiences. We see that Paul was taken up to the 3rd heaven. He said. Whether in the body or out of the body, I do not know. That can happen. God can do anything. Enoch and Elijah were translated into Heaven without seeing death, but that was of God. The Word says Enoch walked with God and was not, because God took him.

Self-willed astral projection is not of God. It is devil assisted. When you are called to a demonic place is definitely not of God. It is a counterfeit spiritual operation that will take you places that you do not and should not want to go to.

Come up here. Who is calling, and what do they want? What "*here*" is requesting you?

You may or may not remember if you've undergone an astral attack since dreams can be *wiped*. If you wake up with scratches on your body but you don't know how they got there, there was most likely an attack. When dark dreams won't go away, that is a sign of dream attack, as well.

They say that when a person dies an angel comes to escort them to Glory. Why do we need an escort? Because there's hell out there and we shouldn't be there without an escort. Outer darkness was never designed for man, neither was hell or the Abyss. There are many places not designed for man. It is not meant for man to be in astral planes, alone. Ever.

Pray— Every power that has summoned my spirit to unknown destinations, let that power die, in the Name of Jesus.

Lord, if I am captive to any evil power, break me out. O God arise and loose me from all evil hands and all evil plans, in the Name of Jesus. *Amen.*

Astral Projected Spirit Spouse

Demons taking sexual liberties as spouses are spirit spouses.

There is a human spirit that is not a demon, but is *demonized* that will astral project to behave as a spirit spouse. As in deliverance a human spirit cannot be gotten rid of the same way that a demonic spirit is cast out, the astral-projected human spirit has to be handled differently than a fallen angel or demon, which is your usual demonic *spirit spouse.* Although there is such a thing as a *physical spirit spouse* the astral spirit spouse is not that either.

Astral sex may mean that you could be having sex with anyone involved in witchcraft–in the dream state, in the sleep--, even a relative. For me, when I finally put two and two together and started praying fervently against this, the Lord showed me **who**. And, He will show you **who** also, if you need to know **who**, once you begin your warfare.

The *who* was someone that I both knew and trusted. He kept a straight face in front of me, his wife, his kids, and everyone else who knew him, because he was well-known and very well respected. I don't know if he still is, and I do not need to know. I've prayed. I've fasted. God's got it from here, at least as it concerns me.

Projected spirit spouse – witch doctors, voodoo priests, occultists, et cetera can use astral projection to have spiritual sex with a victim.

Look who can astral project and do astral sex. That means that the person that God showed me fits in one or more of the above categories, yet he doesn't look, dress, or act like any of those things. This man is like the Wizard of Oz behind a curtain making things happen. He is not what he appears to be.

Could I be mistaken?

Nope.

This is not a masquerade because God showed me by the Holy Spirit, and by reviewing my history since the first time I met him, this man has been obsessed with me, and I'm sure other women too; he has been the source of a lot of the problems and disappointments in my life.

My Father will judge. My job is to repent, ask God for Mercy for myself, and do the spiritual warfare, asking for judgment against my unrepentant enemies.

Astral sex which defiles, and brings on iniquity. The sex is hidden, because it may be wiped from the dream or memory. Dream sex can be so creepy that you wouldn't want to tell anyone about. This is a *spirit spouse*, but it is a human spirit that is astral projecting to victimize you.

That astral projected spirit spouse might be dead, it may be a masquerade—as in a demon that presented as my deceased father-in-law whom I loved, but like a father, not like a husband. *Ewww*. Whatever is presented to you, you have to resist it and overcome it. But because of your sins, or ancestral sins and iniquity, a spirit spouse can be inherited and make you, your children, and your *children's* children their victims as well. Perhaps the appearance of my deceased father-in-law was the spirit spouse from that family bloodline looking for a new victim, and I was married into that bloodline now. Pay attention to spiritual things, Dear Readers.

A Demon by Any Other Name

This chapter is condensed from the chapter of the same name in my book, **Fantasy Spirit Spouse**. It is reprinted here for reference.

A demon by any other name is still a demon.

Prayerlessness and carelessness leave the saved or unsaved open to spirit spouse attack. Other names of spirit spouse are, husband of the night, wife of the night. Nightmares, dream husband, dream wife, incubus, succubus, and Lilith.

Marine spirit spouse – the majority of spirit spouses are from the evil water (marine) kingdom.

Resident spirit spouses are disembodied beings, they believe that humans are their "homes" or house.

Giant spirit spouses are spiritual devil prostitutes. They are remnants from Genesis 6:6.

Serpentine spirit – snake spirit spouses. May appear as ½ human and ½ fish or ½ snake. Can look beautiful as queens or kings with crowns on their heads.

Ancestral spirit spouses pose as living or dead ancestors to the victim. They can be *familiar* and *monitoring spirits* and will sleep with any or everyone in a family.

Physical spirit spouse – when a spirit spouse manifests as a physical human being.

Projected spirit spouse – witch doctors, voodoo priests, occultists, et cetera can use astral projection to have spiritual sex with a victim, (Ecclesiastes 12:6)

Fantasy or *Imagination spirit wife/husband.* https://a.co/d/8YfRxmq

Bloodline spirit spouses (*lust, polygamy spirit spouses, genetic spirit spouses*). Transferred from consensual sex before conception.

Idol spirit spouse – a person attracts generational curses when they worship idol *gods* and end up married to these idol *gods*.

Dwarf spirit husband/wife – some women think these demons are their future children because of their size, but this is not so.

Disembodied spirit spouses are demons with no spiritual bodies.

Strongman spiritual spouse – from generational and family curses.

Leviathan spirit spouses are the old world serpents in charge of water snakes, mermaids, mermen, and merfolk.

Animal spirit spouses. Animals are not meant to be seen in the dream.

Strange man or strange woman spirit spouses physically attack natural spouses.

Old man or old woman spirit spouse usually torment people of younger age with sex in the dream.

Transferred spirit spouse can come from working in deliverance and ministry, et cetera.

Territorial spirit spouses. Every river, house, enclave or subdivision has ruling or territorial demons over those areas.

Hermaphrodite spirit spouses show up as transgendered by whatever means that will work for the evil they plan to inflict on the victim

Hidden spirit spouses don't even show up in the dream. They are not interested in sex in the dream, but they cause disease, tragedies and block success and breakthroughs.

Masquerading spirit spouse is the typical identity theft. They use the face of familiar people so that they will be accepted while you let down your guard and may consent to dream sex

Multiple spirit spouses – when a person experiences more than one sexual partner during the dream.

Incestuous spirit spouse happens in magic, New Age, witchcraft types of homes. It is all demonic.

Witchcraft or warlock spirit spouses – when you consult a witchdoctor you get initiated whether you know it or not. You become a blind witch. That means you are a witch and do not even know it. Period. A spirit spouse is assigned as soon as you visit anyone practicing any of the dark arts.

Celebrity spirit spouse –Memorabilia has familiar spirits attached to them. It's all a masquerade, though.

Transferance spirit spouses – pastors, doctors, intercessors, et cetera should be mightily prayed up so this doesn't happen. Countertransferance is possible also when the deliverance work, pastor, doctor, massage therapist, et cetera transfers their demons to their clients/customers/patients.

Manifested spirit spouses show up first in the dream, but later, they take a human form and show up in the natural.

Graveyard spirit spouse, or necromancer spirit spouses attach to a person from visiting cemeteries, graveyards, going to funerals, etc.

Desert spirit spouse can attach to people who are not prayed up but go to certain areas where demons have been displaced to.

Forest spirit spouse – from a dedicated forest or a dedicated grove, hikers, hunters, et cetera, beware. These demons can follow people home, stalk them and become dream sex partners.

(The original list comprised from Minister Geoff Uzo.)

Grossed out yet? You should be.

*Pray*_____

The spirit transfer transaction that accompanied my unholy first sexual experience, be reversed by the power in the Blood of Jesus, in the Name of Jesus.

The spirit transfer transaction that accompanied any and every sexual attack and any other sexual attacks by a so-called spirit spouse of any description from any origin, be reversed by the power in the Blood of Jesus, in the Name of Jesus.

My virtues for fruitfulness sacrificed on the altar of unholy first sexual experience, take the sacrifice of Christ, and be recovered and restored in the Name of Jesus.

My virtues for fruitfulness sacrificed on the altar of unholy sexual encounters of any kind with any type of spirit spouse, take the sacrifice of Christ and be recovered and restored, in the Name of Jesus.

By the power of the sacrifice of Christ, let the pit that swallowed me because of my unholy first sexual experience vomit and release me now, in the Name of Jesus.

By the power of the sacrifice of Christ, let the pit that swallowed me because of every unholy sexual entanglement with any type of spirit spouse vomit and release me now, in the Name of Jesus.

The evil altar raised by the sacrifice of unholy first sexual experience in my life, marriage and career, collapse and die by the power in the Blood of Jesus and release my breakthroughs in the Name of Jesus.

The evil altar raised by the sacrifice of unholy ritual spirit sex with any so-called spirit spouse at any time, of any type, from any origin, in my life, marriage and career, collapse and die by the power in the Blood of Jesus and release my breakthroughs in the Name of Jesus.

Powers that used my dreams to raise the dark altar of unholy first sexual experience to render me barren for life, die and release my womb/womb of good things, in the Name of Jesus.

Powers that used my dreams to raise the dark altar of unholy sexual encounters with spirit spouse of any type, any kind, at any time, from any source, to render me barren for life, die, DIE, DIE, and release my womb/womb of good things, in the Name of Jesus. *Amen.*

Get Rid of Projected Spirit Spouse

Prayer Against Evil Human Persecutors is from Bride Ministries, Dr. Daniel Duval. Do you need to prove you have spirit spouse before you pray?

No.

If you are praying a prayer that you don't need, God knows. If you are not praying a prayer that you need, one that can help you; God will help you. So pray the following prayer if you want to be free of evil human persecutors, to include *astral projected human spirits* that are roaming about the planet and the universe doing evil under the cloak of invisibility, under the cloak of *I have an alibi—I was at home asleep, lying next to my spouse.*

And they were *lying*, alright.

Prayers Against Human Persecutors

Father, I come before You in the Name of Jesus Christ and I renounce _____, and serve him/her a bill of divorce. I pull up all the hidden documents detailing every covenant, contract, and oath entangling us and command that they be stamped with the Blood of Jesus.

In the Name of Jesus, I pray that Your Heavenly Hosts would be put on assignment to place every part in me that is loyal to _____ on temporary lockdown. I pray that these parts would be put to sleep.

I now deed _____'s territoroy in me over to the kingdom of God and I invite You, Lord Jesus, to take the Throne and rule over this territory with Your Rod of iron.

In the Name of Jesus I now bind all gatekeepers and discover each and every portal access point belonging to _____ (his/her) realm and (his/her) inheritance.

I place the Blood of Jesus upon every portal access point and I seal them with the Holy Spirit. I declare that they are put to sleep and permanently deactivated from this point in time forward.

I take the sword of the Spirit which is the Word of God and I cut myself free from _____ (his/her) realm and (his/her) inheritance in Jesus' Name.

I return every form of counterfeit inheritance inclusive of promised wealth, position, status, calling, ability, power, pride, favors, seed, and any other form of counterfeit inheritance in Jesus' Name. I refuse it and sever myself from it and from this point in time forward I chose to receive my inheritance in Jesus Christ, only.

I renounce all spirit children related to _____ and undo all quantum entanglements involved in their creation. I command their judgment, and the purging of the realms they occupy by judgment through living water. I also reclaim every part of me that has been imprisoned by _____ or in realms related to (him/her).

I release forgiveness by faith to _____ for the evil that (he/she) has done against me. I also discover every part that is a composite of genetic components held together by a cord that binds. I declare that the cords are cut and that each part is separated into its components. I retain my parts and surrender those that do not belong to me. As a man sows, so shall he reap. Vengeance is mine says the Lord.

Lord, I command Your Heavenly Hosts to bind every part of _____ in me and take (him/her) where (he/she) belongs now.

I now take authority over every evil spirit on the inside of me and around me that has been operating under the authority of _____.

I declare that you are discovered, apprehended, bound, pierced through, and thrust out of me for judgment.

I declare that you are being sent to the Abyss for failed assignment.

Lastly, I pray that every spiritual object, tattoo, device, label, marker, power source, grid, or branding placed in or around every part of me by _____ or those under (his/her) authority would be consumed in the Holy Fire of Jesus Christ and totally dissolved. **Amen.**

If you are fighting demons every night, or often, cyclically… regularly, this is why you can't pray a mamby pamby prayer one time and be done with it. This warfare can be intense because the attacks may keep coming, or lay low for a while then bam! show up again to gross you out.

Folks, without spiritual protection, that is a relationship with God and a strong prayer covering, demons can jump in and out of people at will.

Remember the movie *Beetlejuice* – which is not a comedy, by the way? When the people left the house, what did they encounter? Terror. Astral projection is waiting for you if you leave your own house--, that is vacate your physical body. Don't do it.

You can vacate your "house" by hypnosis as well. God says to possess your soul in sanctification and honor. Possessing your soul means keeping it with your body to keep everything intact, not floating about the universe. Further, when you vacate your body, what do you think is happening to your body? You're just napping? Are you semi dead? No, if you've left your own body, a demon or demons can enter it, take up residence in it, and use it while you are not using it. Even when and if you come back to your body, those demons are still there ready to oppress or possess you. That is the goal of demons since they are disembodied, so they try to find a human body to use so they can do things in the Earth that they have no authority to do, except with a human body.

Don't be that for a demon or demons.

Witches can project into your house – they can have a whole meeting there and you may not know they are there – this is also by astral projection.

Just today someone showed me a video of some empty chairs on the back deck of their home that were all facing in the same direction. On camera, it looked as if the *wind* took one chair and spun it around so it now faced the rest of the chairs, as if someone would be seated there to lead a meeting. After a bit, the chair spun around by itself and was put back in its first position.

Meeting over?

There were no visible humans or animals on that deck. It was all caught on camera.

I told her to take authority over her home, her deck, her chairs – everything and send whomever and whatever packing.

She said, *I have to go out there and pray that?*

I said, *NO, you can pray it from right here if you want to, but you can also pray it from inside your house, especially since it is 17 degrees Fahrenheit, outside right now.* If it's too cold outside right now, do threshold prayers.

Calling You Out

I wrote this book for myself and also for you, Dear Reader. I have wondered more than once about astral projection. The term itself makes me think that someone is projecting *to* you.

However, if you are being called out by evil summons to witchcraft covens, satanic circles, or rings, to the marine world, or wherever **evil else**, how is that happening?

It is happening by astral projection--, demon-assisted travel. So, someone or some*thing* can call you out of your own body, call your spirit/soul out while you are sleeping and worse make you do things that you may never do in your waking life, or do things that you don't remember and may never remember, except by the power of the Holy Spirit who will bring all things back to our recall.

How do we get protection from such?

When we vacate our souls that is use drugs, get drunk, get hypnotized, self-hypnotized or believe we are willfully leaving our own bodies, then our bodies can become a dumpster or a cesspool for evil powers to use because we are not in it, ourselves.

Worse, what are we agreeing to out there in the astral world at night while the body is asleep and slobbering? Come on, saints of God!

People leave their sleeping bodies sometimes by evil summons, evil call. Evil, demonic voices give evil commands and the spiritually weak, or spiritually compromised obey. Not only do they obey, they obey what they are told to do once they arrive at a place they are called to. This has always concerned me because what are we really doing or made to do in our "dreams"? Do you really think some entity is going to call you some place and not know what you will do when you get there? Those who are weak of spirit are like putty in evil hands. Build up yourself in the disciplines of the Faith and in reading and studying the Word of God.

They can call out a person, their spirit, or they may call the *spirit* of some good thing in a person's life. Those voices can call out and cage, box, steal, lock away, destroy blessings. Some satanic voices can come from the grave, or from the graveyard. Sometimes it is just a call of the name, sometimes it is the yelling of a name. Some of these voices can come from the water.

A strange voice, and evil summons will summon your spirit or soul to demonic places. Your body is asleep, but the rest of you is not. You may feel as though you are dreaming, but you are actually there. Demonic voices must be taken seriously and silenced by Fire.

Evil summons, demonic voice is a foundational problem. An evil call is for the purpose of grooming you and leading you and ultimately your entire bloodline into bondage. It precedes a demonic attack. Destiny helpers are re-routed. They are lying voices and will say anything to derail you from Godly destiny.

Pray

Witchcraft voices of every kind, environmental, marine, polygamous, and parental witchcraft, scatter against me, in the Name of Jesus.

Every evil voice speaking against me be silenced by the Blood of Jesus.

Every evil voice speaking against my breakthroughs, die by Thunder.

I bless my house and my property, everything that I have stewardship over, in the Name of Jesus. I declare that it is a meeting place for the Angels of God, and I am heavily guarded by Mighty Warrior Angels with swords drawn, in the Name of Jesus.

I declare that if permission or license was given to any entity, power or being that is not of GOD before I started living here; that permission is now revoked by the power in the Blood of Jesus. Anything not of God, must go, it must go, it must go! In the Name of Jesus.

Nakedness in the dream, partial or full – the work of enchanters and diviners--, you will not have success against me in the Name of Jesus. False accusations, satanic delays, lack of helpers, errors, and mistakes, you will not stick in my life, in the Name of Jesus.

Spirit husbands and *spirit wives,* fall down and die, in the Name of Jesus.

Spirit children from any and every quantum entanglement, fall down and die, in the Name of Jesus.

Powers of the night and dream attackers, lose your power, in the Name of Jesus.

Powers of the night, shut your mouth, do not speak to me in the day or night, but especially at night while I am asleep. I am in the Beloved and God gives me sleep and allows me to dwell in safety.

Territorial and environmental powers be mute; you cannot speak sickness, illness, or bewitchment into my life. Bewitch yourself, in the Name of Jesus.

I break the backbone of any power speaking evil into my destiny and life, in the Name of Jesus.

Every agenda of every wicked voice in my waking or dream life, scatter by Thunder, perish by Fire, in the Name of Jesus.

Every strongman holding on to my breakthroughs, release them and then die, in the Name of Jesus.

Lord, if I have been initiated into any evil demonic, repetitive spiritual or natural *service*, I rescind my agreement with such, I revoke all permissions and I destroy any agreements or covenants that put this in place, in the Name of Jesus.

Every satanic siren scaring away my helpers, be silence by the Blood of Jesus.

Any power calling my face, head, or image before evil mirrors, fall down, and die, in the Name of Jesus.

Every evil voice rising up against my life be silenced by Fire, in the Name of Jesus.

The key to my breakthroughs buried beneath the Earth, come forth and locate me by Fire, in the Name of Jesus.

Amen.

Outside the Gate

Sinners and unclean folks were relegated to sit outside the gate to the city in Bible days. They were out there either for the day or for the period of their "uncleanness."

Outside the gate meant not in the presence of other people, but mostly NOT in the presence of the Lord. In the presence of the Lord is where your protection is, so outside means no protection.

Outside the gate there are no policeman or civil servants to protect you; it's like being country-less, or homeless.

Inside the gate the people of God are worshipping, praying, sacrificing, they have access to the Temple and the altars of worship. Inside, is the presence of God, they had access to protection, Mercy, Grace, and the favor of God. If you can't even get into the Gates, how will you get into the Courts of the Lord, or into His Presence.

God does not look on sin, and the devil knows this, so if he can get you to sin, or to make you *look like* you sinned by defiling you, EVEN AGAINST YOUR WILL, as in *spirit spouse rape* – even astral rape – then that is defiled. Defiled means outside of the Gate; out of the presence of the Lord for a designated time. Every morning there are tender mercies. That means that every morning we are forgiven again. So, outside of the gate generally means for a day.

Repent, though. Don't wait until a whole day to repent.

If you are having spirit sex and you're not married, that's fornication. If you are having spirit sex and you are married --, that's not your covenant spouse, so you are an adulterer. This refers to any kind of sex, even unwanted sex. If you *wanted* the sex that's even worse since a person sins when they lust in their heart. Dream sex of any kind is defilement. There are other forms of defilement in the dream as well, but dream sex is definite defilement.

Sex forms covenant. Sex with demons forms evil covenants. Evil covenants allow curses. Curses bring demons to enforce the curses.

To add to the filth, whatever the other demons brought with him or her can be transferred to you. Now you are as guilty as they are. If it is a human, whatever demons they host, can also be transferred to you. You are guilty of everything they are guilty of and you don't even know what all that is. This is worse than the most evil arranged marriage. Where the absolute worst "spouse" (*thing*) in the universe is chosen for you and you have no say so in it.

Lord, have Mercy on us all. We can all clearly see how this is nothing we would ever want and it is something that we should fight with everything that is in us to avoid and get rid of.

REPENT. Repent for everything, even though it may not be your fault, repent of every sin that you can think of considering that sin is sin and one is as bad as all sin.

Repent daily. Repent often because the unclean could not enter a holy place where worship, and sacrifice were offered--, where sins were dealt with. Outside the Gate means you can't even get in to REPENT.

Are You *Attracting* It?

Here's what they like; these are some of the things that attract spirit spouse: your blessings, your prosperity, your success, your wealth, your breakthroughs. There is no way any of us should avoid those blessings, therefore we must guard them and keep them for our life and for godliness.

These also draw spirit spouse: Evil covenants, idolatry—when you start it, or stop it improperly; idols demand their worship. Ancestral curses, evil foundation, generational curses, familial curses, individual curses, works of the flesh—especially sex sins--, masturbation, fornication, adultery, sexual perversions of any description. Evil human agents may *send* a person a spirit spouse.

The *spirits* in you influence everything about you, from how you think to how you dress to how you wear your nails and hair, and all that makeup. If the *spirits* that are in you feel as if they married you, then you have one or more spirit spouses. If they don't marry you, but open the door for others by influencing you to attract spirit spouse if the *spirits* that are in you are **supposed** to attract *spirit spouse* or mark you for spirit spouse. When you were first and subsequently defiled that is when those *spirits* entered your soul.

How do you get rid of spirit spouse? Get those attracting, controlling or boss *spirits* out of your soul. Deliverance from spirit spouse (s) Changing the way you dress may be a start.

- If the way that I dress or style my hair, nails, or makeup has made me into a strange altar, Blood of Jesus, let that altar die, in the Name of Jesus.

You are a strange altar? Could be. You shouldn't be, but you could be.

Spirit spouse loves super sexy outfits, tight clothes, short skirts, and low cut tops. They love hair extensions and weaves, nails that look like eagle's talons. If God hates what you're wearing; if it is a perversion--, then the devil will run to that. That's the kind of stuff that makes you into a strange altar. They like certain music, dances, fragrances, and even certain foods and beverages. They come running because it is as though you're putting out a offering for them. Come on, milk & cookies for Santa – that's a food offering to an idol. No, it is not harmless.

Still, if they like all the "hot stuff" that doesn't mean that a librarian who looks and dresses like a librarian can't have a spirit spouse, but the walking altars, as they say in bad court scenes – are just asking for it. Demons love certain things, certain styles, certain colors. Saints of God – the evil marine kingdom runs the cosmetic, hair, fashion, music, movie, and beauty industries.

Your outfits and hairstyles can mark you. BUT like the chicken and the egg conundrum, which came first? Were you defiled one night when you were whatever age and then immediately or slowly after that you changed your appearance? Or were you dressed like a hooker before you were marked in the spirit as one? Pray, ask God, then listen to the Holy Spirit.

Hair bundles for weaves and extensions, wigs—even the ones that boast all natural hair is basically cursed. Where does that hair come from? Sometimes it is gotten off of dead people. If you look closely, the all "virgin" or all natural hair has grey hairs in it. How old do you think the person that donated it was? Did the person who allegedly donated it even *know* that they donated hair?

In some wigs, the younger hair is in the front and more visible, and the older person's hair is in the back. Look closely, you will see different textures, that hair was not all donated from the same person.

The hair is enchanted over. And, sadly it is the rage for people from all kinds of people groups. Wigs and hair extensions have been used since time began. In the 60s women used hair pieces to create a beehive hairstyle. The modern hair weave was invented by a Black woman, Christina Jenkins who created it by weaving live and commercial hair together. Whatever the source of hair extensions and wig hair, those countries and continents are **not** primarily Christian and many times the area of donation has a very heavy witchcraft culture. Do you want witches' hair on your head, polluting your glory?

Indian hair is sacrificed to their idol *gods*. Why then, would you put that on or ATTACH it to your head, covering and corrupting your real

GLORY, looking like a caricature of yourself? Ask God what He thinks about this, in your case.

If someone can be affected by wearing some one else's jewelry, their clothes – how much more their hair, every day or day after day for weeks and months, maybe even years? IF the person whose hair you were wearing was not Christian, and may already had a spirit spouse, you just inherited their spiritual menagerie.

Rainbow colored hair is a fad from the evil marine kingdom. Attracting demons. When you wear their stuff, you *mark* yourself as one of theirs so they think they have rights to you. All rights; even sexual rights. These styles attract spirit spouse.

How It Happened

I want to share how I came to know that I was under attack by an astral spirit spouse.

There was feeding in the dream. There was sex in the dream. Both were very unusual dreams for me, but I'm not sure how long that had been happening since I had gone through a short season of not recalling my dreams at all and that had to stop. So I had prayed to remember my dreams and the Lord honored my prayers.

In addition to that I woke up with scratches similar to those pictured on my arm. I showed them to more than one person and they tried to explain it away by saying that I scratched myself. But you can look up case after case where people are waking up with similar or different scratches in places that they cannot even reach.

Spirit spouse. Those marks are to mark you and defile you. **Don't do nothing about it.**

This undeniable, and inexcusable symptom began my research and study of the subject with fastings, prayers and searching for deliverance.

The purpose of astral projecting is to stalk a person, oppress, harass, depress, sabotage, accuse, gossip, deceive, rape them, abuse them, steal, kill, destroy. None of this is for your pleasure and there is never *free* sex. Immediately prayer treat dreams where you are eating or having sex with **any one** in the dream. In the dream you are in the spirit. Spirits don't eat. Spirits should not have sex, (Matthew 22:30a)

An astral projector may be very bold, if they are triangulated with the sun, or very sneaky if they are triangulated with the moon. You may know them, and they will sit right there in front of you doing their evil thing. You may think that they are sleeping or dozing off--, but they are not. *Where have they gone?* That wizard or warlock is astral projecting, doing whatever to whomever while you believe he is still right there with you and the rest of the group you are with.

Or, have they been summoned somewhere and sleep wave has descended upon them? A witch, warlock, or wizard is not their own; they have to answer to higher evil powers. They, too could be summoned somewhere. Pray the Holy Spirit will tell you and will tell you when it's time and how to get out of there.

Watch what you are doing for and with people – an *evil exchange* may be taking place if, for example, they want you and only YOU to do a certain thing for them or with them. When a grown person is acting like a two-year-old having a tantrum, insisting you must do that or the other, and it can only be you and it has to be now— watch out for witchcraft! Be prayed up – stay prayed up.

In my twenties – I'm trying to sleep – I feel the bed go down and there is no one in the bed, in the room, or in my apartment but me. I convinced myself that I'm imagining things, but it was scary, but I prayed as much as I could, as much as I knew how to at that time. I called on the name of Jesus. Jesus. Jesus.

I don't know what happened in months and weeks after that. I dreamt a lot regularly, but I had no dreams of sex in the sleep or in the dream. I had a spiritual affliction, more than one, actually but the ones we are talking about are the spirit spouse. I didn't know I had it, and didn't even know that there was such a thing. Where did it come from? If it is a family spirit spouse, it followed me to college, it followed me from home.

If it was sent by the scorned ex, or the scorned ex's parents, or the girlfriend that the guy you're dating is cheating on, and you don't even know he's got a real girlfriend, or another girlfriend, or a wife--, but she learns about you, and makes you her target, that's a serious problem, as well. Lord help! If a spirit spouse was <u>sent</u> to you, that's another whole thing.

I recall sleep paralysis, once or so in my 20's. The bed went down one or two nights, as I recall, and then it either stopped, or was *wiped*, and I forgot about it. I didn't even know what a wiped dream meant or that it was possible. Like most people I thought I was spiritually cool if I was aware of myself and my dreams, went to church and respected thunderstorms. I didn't think much past myself or that there was a real invisible world out there.

For a couple of months, I would fly in dreams. I was oblivious that this was a devil attack or that it had any bearing on my real life or future. **Don't you be ignorant as well**.

These attacks were to defile a person for spiritual marriage. The evil *spirit* or giant sons of God (Genesis 6:6) cannot marry a regular, normal human—that human must be **defiled** first. I call it *slimed*. If you are undefiled the demons can't touch you. If you're slimed, you're their target.

During that season of my life, in my youth, I said a prayer or two and as far as I know it stopped. For the next years or so, after that, I had flying dreams – as soon as I close my eyes to sleep, I'm flying – not dizzy, but flying. It happened regularly, so as I investigated that in the wrong places, I was told wrong information and believed it was OK, or that I was special. Again, I was young and dumb.

One of the purposes of this book is so you, at any age, are not ignorant of the devil's devices.

As a teenager I was saved and Baptized Baptist – I thought that was all there was because the pastor's sermons went on repeat. He preached the same thing every week—salvation, and had an altar call. If I was already saved, then wouldn't I think that I have this "God thing" figured out – that's all there is? Getting saved. Every week. It was like Blues Clues, so I felt if I missed a Sunday, I didn't miss anything.

And, I didn't, at least in that place. Still, I knew there had to be more. The purpose of church had to be more than to just show up because you're supposed to. Sit still for a couple of hours. Sing the three hymns on the board, speak to the others at church, and feel better when you leave.

If you didn't come to church, people would judge you—that's what I thought.

Defiling spirit spouses come to steal from you. Your having nice things attracts demons--, the ones who are on assignment to steal from you. You probably have met people like that and steering clear of them – they can't stand to see you have anything. Do not tell them you have a new car, house, boyfriend girlfriend—, nothing -- but especially things of monetary value-- they will be eaten up with what looks to be jealousy but they take it to a whole level, because if the *spirit of the emptier* is working in them, they will stop at nothing trying to drain every good thing from your life. Stop putting all your business on social media.

The *spirit of the emptier,* no matter what they themselves have, they don't want to see you with anything. They want to take you from grace to disgrace. From Grace to grass. From a place of honor to dishonor. From success to failure …poverty. Spirit spouses work with them, for them, or they **are** part of that evil force.

The kingdom of God suffereth violence and the violent take it by force.

Spirit spouse is coming to steal, kill, and destroy, through sex. It's goal is NOT SEX. You may think it is because we humans think that others – especially men want sex from us ladies. Lusty men are on assignment whether they know it or not. ***Through*** sex the *spirits* and powers that run them get what they want from their victims. Your spiritual gifts, your talents, everything. They behave as an emptier, to leave you empty so you look and feel as though you are not succeeding in life.

In my 20's, I was in college. The stupidest things in the world would happen to me at school, and most of it was related to *paperwork,* credentials, and identification. In my second year of school, the Registrar's office decided that I wasn't an American citizen. I had been a citizen all the previous year and had never been out of the country before in my entire life.

This is demonic. BUT, if you are not spiritual and do not think spiritually about issues that arise you may go to the common denominator and scream the same thing that others are complaining about. I'm Black; they're discriminating against me. *Really*? I'm a woman; they are discriminating against me.

No, this is a spiritual issue. Yes, those "discriminating" may be pawns of the devil, but the problem is foundational, and it is spiritual.

He also that is slothful in his work is brother to him that is a great waster. (Prov 18:9)

Some signs that the *waster spirit* is at work in our life are as follows:
- Hard work doesn't turn in to what you thought it would.
- Always losing money—even when God answer your prayers. One bad

thing after another happens to drain you of money when you have any.

God is about wise stewardship; it is one of the reasons man was put on Earth. God loved Joseph because he was prudent; that is, he was a wise steward.

The Israelites did evil in the LORD's sight. So the LORD handed them over to the Midianites for seven years. The Midianites were so cruel that the Israelites made hiding places for themselves in the mountains, caves, and strongholds. Whenever the Israelites planted their crops, marauders from Midian, Amalek, and the people of the east would attack Israel,
(Judges 6:1-3)

This was the work of the *waster spirit*. Wasters will let you work and work and work and will then raid your progress. Spirit spouses enter your life to waste your progress and divert or steal your destiny; they must go. Some cultures believe that the spirit spouse is a good thing; it is NOT! I seem to be oppressed by one or more for years. God has blessed me in spite of that, but I have not gotten anything good from a spirit spouse. They promise good things, but it is the opposite—they come to take from you. **They must go!**

The Importance of Destiny

Why is your destiny so important? The difference between hearing from God, *Well done, good and faithful servant,* or *Get away from me, you worker of iniquity* is the fulfillment of destiny--, or not. It is the difference between gaining an eternal crown, or having no crown. Fulfilling destiny determines if you have jewels in your eternal crown and what kind and number of jewels.

Fulfilling destiny is important to prosper your bloodline.

Prospering the plan of God for mankind is the overarching purpose of us all being here and performing our little purposes in the grand scheme of things.

Think of a relay race; right now, you've got the baton. If you don't do the part that you're supposed to do in that race, the last runner's work will not be in vain, and so that the next runner can succeed. In regard to your bloodline, and relative to your destiny, what do you plan for your children to do? What of their success? If they've got to start where you started and didn't finish--, if you don't end up where you're supposed to end up, your children will start *behind* the starting mark for their lives. They will have to start **behind** the God-ordained starting line instead of *at* it. They've got to do double the work—, what yours and theirs? You're not selfish, right? So, then their children will start out behind, as well. Without doing your part, you potentially create a family of failures.

Well done, good and faithful servant. Will God say that to you? Will God be able to say that to your children? How is it possible if what they've been created for and purposed to do they never do? If your children are failures, God will judge them, as well as you.

God visits to the third and fourth generation of those that love Him and up to 14 generations of those who are not serving Him.

God judges.

God judges the entire bloodline, collectively. If your children remember God, then that is accounted to you. If they don't, that is counted against you. If you're handing your child the family baton and they don't know why or what the baton is for, then you haven't done your purpose and your job.

Whomever let a spirit spouse into your bloodline, or other evil *spirits* like *emptiers* and *wasters* are bringing the whole bloodline down. Things happen, but whoever is letting demons into the bloodline and not doing anything about it – that is at least trying to get rid of them, and get deliverance is jeopardizing themselves as well as the entire bloodline. To discover that you have a spirit spouse and do nothing about it means spirit spouse will continue into your generations doing damage, blocking and stealing blessings so your family is not just uncomfortable, but they are not able to serve God. The entire bloodline will be at dire risk.

If nothing is being done to get rid of spirit spouse is it because humans keep sexual things a secret? Is it because humans keep sexual secrets a secret? Spirit, astral sex is a dirty secret, but it is not yours to carry. It is demonic and you need deliverance. There are many ways to get deliverance but it is only through God, His Word, and by the Holy Spirit with fasting and praying.

Do your part so the relay race of your family will be victorious. While you're at it, while you're in the race, since you've got the baton, why not knock the devil upside the head, metaphorically speaking?

Relationships

I have always been choosy about whom I dated, but the VERY wrong thing I did in dating was that I was applied worldly rules to dating instead of Biblical laws. That was bad, but being **in** the world and certainly *of* it, by my wrong behavior, I rationalized that if I didn't do what everyone else was doing I'd never get or keep a boyfriend. No matter the relationship, something would happen to break us up.

Why?

Sin. Why would I ever think I'd get Godly results from ungodly behavior?

And, what else? Spirit spouse. A thing I knew absolutely nothing about at the time, but I now believe that my life was on the timeline of a *spirit spouse.* **And it sucked.**

In those days I fasted a lot because food was not that interesting to me. I only chose to eat to keep from getting stomach cramps, so I'd eat one meal one day and then two meals the next. It was comfortable for me to split up one day's meals over two days—breakfast and dinner one day and then only lunch the next. Not to lose weight, I just wasn't that interested in food. And involuntary fast is not a dedicated fast, and that can be dangerous. There is such a thing as an *evil fast*.

I am saying that dedicated fasts are crucial in getting deliverance, especially from spirit spouse. At that time I knew nothing about fasts or anything else. I just knew I was Baptist and going to Heaven way, way in the future.

Time goes by.

Years later, all the sleep drama is forgotten. The sleep paralysis, bed depression and flying in the dreams are all long forgotten. I got married. I thought it was a forever marriage, but one day my husband just turned on me. Of course, he was manipulative and sneaky, and I hate both of those behaviors and didn't tolerate them or turn a blind eye on them. For this reason, I suppose he felt trapped because he wanted to be married but behave as a man who is not married. I'd have no part of that. So, we split apart.

But the reason I mention him is because at the end of our relationship he wrote me a note that I wish I had kept because I'd reprint it in this book. The note asked me to please divorce him, "lest he die."

Lest he die -- , I laughed so hard at his Shakespearean vernacular, but now that years have passed, I wonder if he had a dream that if we didn't break up with me that he would *die*. That is the kind of stuff that a spirit spouse would do; it hates the natural spouse and works diligently to get rid of them. Spirit spouse can cast into a dream and scare, threaten, and manipulate a human.

After he wrote that note he either became full of fear, or acted as if he was very fearful. I was still praying to God for our marriage and on his behalf--, that is until the Lord stopped me, and I could only pray in the spirit after that. His own mother became fearful, I wonder to this day what he may have said to her, or if she also had some demonic dream, or if she was afraid of her son (he's a big bully), but she's gone on to Glory.

The Patterns

About three years ago, after the three long scratches on my body, it was now time to start mapping this thing out; it is time to study patterns.

I had been having sex dreams, but now a face was being assigned to the attacker. One night I played a strong warfare video on loop overnight, ***The Crying Blood of Jesus*** **https://www.youtube.com/watch?v=uWjlYacNQs8** . In the dream a voice said, *"Turn that off. Your husband is here."* I woke up the next morning, remembering that, and I was appalled. **My God of Mercy! I really have a spirit spouse. And, I recognized the voice! It was a person. This was astral projection. I KNOW this person! I've been knowing this person FOR YEARS.**

I made sure to play that prayer and others overnight on loop for months and months after that while I sought more knowledge on this and deliverance.

It is very difficult to fight the spirit of a human person showing up in the dream for sex, but really is after something else—who am I kidding, they are after **EVERYTHING** that's good in your life.

Evil exchange? They are not beyond that. They are there to steal destiny. I could be on the verge of a creative idea, a breakthrough or blessing, but then have a spirit spouse sex dream the night before and boom goes the dynamite. Everything would blow up and not in a good way. Since then, I've come to believe that this astral projecting evil human may have done a money ritual and is hitting up as many females as possible because he is obsessed with money, brags about how much he has, but also begs professional WOMEN for things and stuff all the time, in the natural.

RUN!

I did.

PRAY!

I do, and I am. I will not let up.

I don't recall many spirit spouse, sex type dreams while I was married before. We had sex every night; yes, every night – because he wanted to father a child. BUT I later found out that he was using porn as his "fluffer" so any of you can guess what kinds of demons were in that bedroom with us. God wasn't in that mess.

Regarding that ex-husband, his own spirit spouse(s) could have turned him against me. We both could have had spirit spouses or even more than one each. On top of that, the spirit spouses are fighting, but we are the humans in the Earth realm walking it out and suffering.

But now, a few years ago, I realize that the one that the Holy Spirit has shown me is the evil human astral projecting spirit spouse could have been in this whole mix while both of us were totally unaware. Because since then I've found out this human never wanted me to marry the man I married.

A few years into the marriage, the husband's father died. Within a day or two, one night in a dream, his "father" appeared to me in a sexual way. I said, within the dream, *"What are you doing here? You're dead, and the dead know nothing."* The apparition turned to heavy dust, like metallic rice pellets and went through the floor like it was pulled through the floor. I suppose, back to hell where it came from? I say, **Failed Assignment.**

I never told anyone. The man was grieving, how could I tell him such a thing about his father in a *dream*? But it was horrifying.

Spirit spouse, *monitoring spirit, familial spirits,* astral projection by an evil human agent, -- all this is foundational problems so ancestral curses and powers are involved as well. None of us are sin-free, but within that marriage I certainly tried to walk upright before the Lord.

Women, you know how sometimes we ask if there's a target on our backs, or if we have a creep magnet or something? The man's dead father showed up --, I look back now and ask, Was I *marked* for spirit spouse? There was no other reason for such a thing to happen. Saints of God do not let the enemy mark you and have you out there in those spiritual streets doing Lord knows what!

Toward the end of that marriage, I found under three locks, a locked closet, a locked cabinet and a locked briefcase – a briefcase FULL of pictures of scantily clad women – like 200 pictures--, in our "marital" home. You can guess what *spirits* also lived in that house, in that soul.

I don't know how long he had been collecting them, but I could clearly see he was not planning to let them go. Soft or hard porn is a sure spirit spouse invitation.

Lord, have Mercy. I'd say we both were a hot mess.

Cut Soul Ties

While still in that marriage, a cat ran at my car in a dream, it didn't get in, but I remembered its eyes--- they were the eyes of a hostile church member, one with whom my ex often flirted with. Yup, that's a attempted witchcraft dream.

Without forgiveness I can feel a certain kind of way toward that church person, whether she knows it or not. Unforgiveness creates soul ties. Soul ties are bad. The cat didn't get to me because at that time I said I was living as sin-free as possible. Whatever collections of *spirits* were in my then-husband, God showed me Mercy and I believe most of them didn't transfer to me.

However, you can have soul ties with anything, a building, a song, food, people, – they don't have to be people that you are having sex with. You can be soul tied with church members--, family members, coworkers – anyone, for good or bad reasons. When you leave a place or a relationship, as God directs, break soul ties.

The enemy can use anyone; even people who do not know they are being used--, as *monitoring spirits* – people could be telling your business to the devil all night long, if summoned to a coven or an evil council--, and not even aware of it. Others invite you to sin to defile you or get you to defile yourself, then the devil can get in.

There is nothing the devil can do in your life unless it first goes through a human. Often that is a relative or someone who is close to you.

Cut soul ties. When it's time to move on, and God says the same, shake the dust and be sure to cut soul ties. A soul tie is an evil covenant. And evil covenant allows a curse to alight. Curses are enforced by demons. A spirit spouse is a demon.

Break all soul ties.

Unclean Spirits

Whether forced or not, having sex with a demon transfers a lot of evil to a human.

What is the *body count* of a DEMON?

What is the body count of a person who is so pleased and proud to go into the night and attack, that is rape men and/or women because they *can*. Do you think they only did it once? Do you think you're the only one? OF COURSE, not!

Do you have strange STD's and you haven't even been with anyone? You get meds for an STD, but the meds don't seem to be working. These odd discharges are resistant to regular medicine. People, astral sex is sex with demons, it is disgusting, and it transfers disease to humans-- inexplicable, unexplainable diseases.

And you will be spiritually defiled. If you don't realize it, do anything about it, or know that you can do something about it... or how to do something about it, you will stay defiled and if defiled, you are defile-able--- again and again. That makes you a prostitute in the spirit. It puts an evil mark on you, making you a target, singling you out for sexual attacks in the dream or sleep, that is, in the spirit. And it destroys your life and happiness in the natural.

Being defiled puts you outside the GATE, outside the Presence of the Lord, , far away from God, worship, sacrifice, repentance and deliverance.

Do you think the *same* spirit spouse is coming each time? If, that's more and more evil transference! Now there are even more hidden sins.

DEFILED means to make unclean; to render foul or dirty; in a general sense. To make impure; to render turbid. To soil or sully; to tarnish; as reputation. We worry about reputation unless we think no one will know, then as humans, we don't seem to care. People of God, someone always knows; God always knows. The devil set the whole thing up to trap you, so he is watching and keeping a record as well. You have a reputation in the spirit that is even more important than the one you have here on Earth with your fellow humans.

To defile means to pollute; to make *ceremonially* unclean, (Leviticus 22). In the Old Testament, an Israelite would become defiled or ceremonially unclean for any violation of God's commandments.

An unclean spirit is SPIRITUALLY DEAD, it has NO life of God in it, therefore, it is defiled, and we should have nothing to do with it, much less let it touch us or have sex with it.

He that toucheth the dead body of any man shall be unclean seven days,
(Numbers 19:11)

Shechem *defiled* Dinah, (Genesis 34); he raped her. To defile also means, *to taint*, to corrupt; to render impure with sin.

Idol gods are demons; demons are idols.

Defile not yourselves with the idols of Egypt.
(Ezekiel 20)

If we're living an immoral life we are fully *of* the world when we should only be in it. Additionally, people that we have relationships with, have their own pasts. Some of them may be evil human agents, knowingly, or unknowingly. These agents are defiled in the utmost and most terrible way. This is reason enough to not pursue the bad boys, or the bad girls. Spiritual body count is a really good reason.

By deception, or for *fun,* living the party life, people defile themselves, out here in these streets. Know that when they sleep with you, the Lord will see you two as having become one. The spiritual transference of demons is real, folks.

If you have been attacked in the night by any spirit spouse, -- any type from the list of types of spirit spouses, consider them **unclean**. Especially if attacked by an astral rapist—a human spirit, you must consider that they are **the worst of the worst**. They have probably committed every possible sin and are probably reprobate. They didn't *accidentally* astral travel, or accidentally attack or rape you. They knew exactly what they were doing, unless under satanic programming or remote control.

- Lord, have Mercy on me and declare judgment on every astral projecting spirit spouse, in the Name of Jesus.
- Let the power of every astral projecting spirit spouse DIE, in the Name of Jesus.

Suit Up for Warfare

Lord, have Mercy on me, a sinner. I repent today for all my sins and the sins of my ancestors. Please remove all iniquity from me and my bloodline that I may live and that my children and my *children's* children may live, in the Name of Jesus.

Lord, break me free from anything evil that I have knowingly or unknowingly signed up for or have been initiated into, in the Name of Jesus.

Lord, if I am a blind witch, warlock, or wizard, deliver me today, in the Name of Jesus.

Any demons picked up or agreed to by astral travel either successful or attempted soul travel, Lord have Mercy and deliver me today, in the Name of Jesus.

Any wicked power calling forth my spirit, you are a liar, die, in the Name of Jesus.

Every *familiar spirit* assigned against me, die by Fire, in the Name of Jesus.

My spirit man, reject every witchcraft call, in the Name of Jesus.

Every power bewitching my star, you're a liar, fall down and die, in the Name of Jesus.

Power invoking my spirit to wander, let the Thunder of God destroy you, in the Name of Jesus.

Any astral demons monitoring me, die by Fire, in Jesus' Name.

I withdraw my glory from the astral world, in the Name of Jesus.

Every astral projection into my life and destiny. Go back to your sender, in the Name of Jesus.

Every evil bird flying for my sake, fall down dead from the sky, and be roasted by Fire, in the Name of Jesus.

Every agenda of the enemy for my life, your time is up; die by Fire, in the Name of Jesus.

Every arrow of *familiar spirits*, backfire, in Jesus' Name.

Powers assigned to possess me, die by the power in the Blood of Jesus.

My spirit, reject every witchcraft call, in the Name of Jesus.

I frustrate every exchange of my virtues, in the Name of Jesus.

I deliver my soul from every bewitchment of astral attack, in the Name of Jesus.

Every spell or enchantment programmed against me by astral powers, be destroyed, in the Name of Jesus.

Spiritual marriage with *familiar spirits*, ancestral powers, or family *idols*, be destroyed now and forever, in the Name of Jesus.

I burn every certificate, every document, every emblem and token of a spiritual marriage and I nullify any covenant with any unclean spirit, demon, devil or evil, astral projecting human agent, in the Name of Jesus.

Blood of Jesus, destroy every *familiar spirit* manipulation fashioned against me, in the Name of Jesus.

The weapons of *familiar spirits* turn against them, in the Name of Jesus.

Every *familiar spirit* stealing my virtues, release them and die, in Jesus' Name.

Every evil, defiling deposit in my spirit, soul and body be flushed out by the Blood of Jesus, in the *Name* of Jesus.

Every stranger in my body, in my soul, in my ministry, life and calling, business, marriage, and family, get out, in the Name of Jesus.

By Fire, I destroy every soul tie between me and the occult kingdom and witchcraft kingdom, in Jesus' Name.

Let the Thunder and Lightning of the Lord scatter all the forces of the enemy, in the Name of Jesus.

Any astral ritual done on my soul to explore my virtues, or for any other reason, roast to ashes, in Jesus' Name. East Wind of God, blow them away, in Jesus' Name.

Heavenly Hosts, destroy every witch, warlock, or wizard using astral travel to monitor, observe, or attack me, in the Name of Jesus.

Any identification mark of the occultic upon my body, spirit, soul, or life, be washed off by the Blood of Jesus.

Every invisible enemy that is roaming around my premises at night, or at any time to observe or subdue me, be exposed and be ignited by Fire, in Jesus' Name.

Fire of the Holy Ghost, destroy their witchcraft covens and scatter them to desolation, in Jesus' Name.

Fire of God consume all those planning evil food and beverage for me, in the Name of Jesus.

Fire of God, burn to ashes, the agenda of eaters of flesh and drinkers of blood, in the Name of Jesus.

Let all the strongholds of the serpent and scorpion in my household receive the Thunder of God and be dismantled, in the Name of Jesus.

I bind and paralyze any witchcraft agent leaving their physical body in order to attack me. Lord rule over them with the Rod of Fire by the authority in the Name of Jesus.

Any power that has vowed never to stop afflicting my life, receive the judgement of God's Fire, in the Name of Jesus.

Lord, let every astral projection attack fashioned against me and my family, backfire 7-fold, in the Name of Jesus.

Satanic stargazers monitoring the star of my destiny for evil, receive God's judgment of blindness, in the Name of Jesus.

Every satanic out of the body summons to pollute my destiny fail woefully, in the Name of Jesus.

My spirit man do not obey witchcraft instructions, in the Name of Jesus.

Any evil, lying prophecy against my life and family backfire, in the Name of Jesus.

Every astral travel arrangement made to cage me and my original life, be canceled now, in the Name of Jesus.

Witchcraft coven enchantment aimed at sending my spirit man on an evil assignment is rendered null and void by the power in the Blood of Jesus.

Every enchantment spell, incantation, divination, and all forms of voodoo fashioned against my spirit man be deprogrammed and dismantled, in the Name of Jesus.

I tender the sacrifice of Jesus Christ and the Blood of Jesus against any and every satanic ritual offered against me in the spirit realm, in the Name of Jesus.

Lord, let any witchcraft entity that attends any coven meetings against my life, be struck by the Holy Ghost Fire.

Every astral projecting demonic, spiritual, or evil human agent, crash land on the way to my house and receive the judgment of God's Fire, in the Name of Jesus.

Forget my name, lose my location, in the Name of Jesus.

Any Satanic spirit on assignment to possess my life, fail, in the Name of Jesus. Lord, cut off the wickedness of the wicked, in the Name of Jesus.

Every authority given to any demonic power or evil human agent to do me harm of any kind, be revoked by the breaking of every evil covenant by the power in the Blood of Jesus.

Satanic agenda over my life be defeated, now, by the power of the Holy Ghost, by the power, in the Name of Jesus.

Lord, let the power in the Blood of Jesus neutralize, and expose and paralyze every invisible agent of darkness that has been instructed to monitor me, day and night, in the Name of Jesus.

Lord, let the power in the Blood of Jesus neutralize and expose and paralyze every invisible agent of darkness that has been assigned to attack me at any time, in the Name of Jesus.

I command the judgment Fire of God on any evil altar, ministering against my life and family, in the Name of Jesus.

I set ablaze any satanic ancestral or any other ladder that the enemy is using or has used against my life, against my destiny. They are consumed and destroyed by Holy Ghost Fire, in the Name of Jesus.

By Holy Ghost. Fire, by the power of the Holy Ghost, we block the path of all my spiritual enemies from attending witchcraft coven meetings, in the Name of Jesus.

Lord, break the power of their worship to their evil powers, in the Name of Jesus.

In the Name of Jesus, any satanic assembly drawing strength from the stars to launch an attack against your life, be judged and scattered unto desolation by the Lord of Hosts.

Lord, let my spirit man be covered by the Blood of Jesus and is not summonable, let it not be attackable, in Jesus' Name.

I am transfused by the Blood of Jesus and my blood cannot be shed, in the Name of Jesus.

I shall not be the prey of satanic astral projection. (X3)

My body, soul, spirit – Lord let no part of me answer an evil summons, ever, in the Name of Jesus.

Any form of affliction programmed into the heavenlies against my life, backfire, in the Name of Jesus.

By the power of the Holy Ghost, any witchcraft agent coming up against me, shall not return alive, in the Name of Jesus. Lord, cut off the wickedness of the wicked. Cut their lives short, in the Name of Jesus.

Any spiritual spy commissioned to monitor my life for evil, be crushed by the Rock of Ages, in the Name of Jesus.

Every conscious or unconscious covenant with the Queen of the Coast that is exposing me to satanic attacks and summons is broken now by the power in the Blood of Jesus.

Household witchcraft, stand down, stand down against my life and destiny. Get out of my business, stop cooperating with my enemies, or receive the wrath of God Almighty, in the Name of Jesus.

Any witch, warlock, wizard, or sorcerer embarking on an evil trip against me, I burn your routes by judgment and with the Fire of the Lord, in the Name of Jesus.

Every spiritual gate servicing witchcraft operation against me, be shut now with this prayer, by the power in the Blood of Jesus.

Whatever is within or around me, attracting spiritual attacks to your life, you are a worker of iniquity; depart from me now, in the Name of Jesus.

Right Hand of God, arise and smite the mouth of any satanic priest or priestess hired against me, in the Name of Jesus.

Every Satanic agent disguised to manipulate my spirit man through astral projection attacks, be exposed and defeated, in the Name of Jesus.

Any demonic voice calling my name or issuing evil summons to me, be struck mute by Thunder Lightning of God. Be discomfited with many arrow and rendered mute for all eternity, in the Name of Jesus.

By the power in the Blood of Jesus, we seal up their dimensional access point for attacks against me, in the Name of Jesus.

Warrior angels of God, chastise any power invoking witchcraft, astral projection against me, in the Name of Jesus.

Any child of the devil embarking on astral travel to consult witchcraft covens, marine temples, or dark powers in the heavenlies against my life, fail woefully, in the Name of Jesus.

Any demonic personality disguised as an Angel of light in order to access my life shall not prosper. We command them to go into everlasting captivity, in the Name of Jesus.

Sun, do not smite me by day, nor the moon by night. Stars, do not listen to coven instructions against me, but turn those words against the enchanters in the Name of Jesus.

Astral projection attack is forever defeated in against me under the threat of severance of the silver cord, in the name of Jesus.

Lion of the Tribe of Judah, the Root of David, roar against every witchcraft, astral travel, up against my life, in the Name of Jesus.

Lion of Judah pursue and devour every witchcraft pursuer assigned against my destiny and my life, in the Name of Jesus,

Arise, O Lord, Lion of Judah, arise and set me free from the shackles of witchcraft, wizardry, occultism and astral projection and projectionists, in the Name of Jesus.

Lion of Judah roar and defend me against every Satanic assignment against me, in the Name of Jesus.

Lion of Judah roar for me; drown out every demonic voice, and evil summons after my divine destiny, in the Name of Jesus.

Mighty Lion of the Tribe of Judah, put fear in the heart of all my enemies, that they flee from me, in the Name of Jesus

The Lord will put your dread and fear upon the enemies of your soul.

Satanic lions be trampled by the Lion of the Tribe of Judah; let your place of habitation be devoured, in the Name of Jesus.

The astral travel plans of territorial evil powers against your life be frustrated and defeated, in the Name of Jesus.

Any authority that I have given any witch, warlock, wizard, or any power to enter my house, environment, business, or life, be revoked now by the power in the Blood of Jesus.

I pray for Mercy. Lord, let Your judgment Fire burn them to ashes, in the Name of Jesus.

The Lion of Judah defend Your interest in my life and family, in the Name of Jesus.

Lion of Judah, deliver me from mysterious spiritual battles and all witchcraft, in the Name of Jesus.

Astral projection attack fashioned against my life Cease and Desist under threat of severance of your silver cord, in the Name of Jesus.

Mighty warrior angels of God surround me, my house and my environment with swords drawn. Defend me from every astral projector, in the Name of Jesus.

Be ready with Fire Swords to defend me from every evil pursuer and every evil summons to evil locations and destinations with evil purpose, in the Name of Jesus.

Lord, let Your fear come upon every entity and even human spirit assigned to attack my life or any part of my life, in the Name of Jesus.

Lion of Judah, arise and avenge me of my adversaries in the Name of Jesus.

Every spirit spouse of any source, origin, or variety become impotent in the Name of Jesus.

Every astral traveler with intent to attack me in the day, in the night, in the sleep, in the dream – at any time, become permanently impotent, in the Name of Jesus.

Command the Night

https://www.youtube.com/watch?v=73M0Q696SAI

Father, I come before You tonight in prayer. I come to command the night.

I enter into Your gates with Thanksgiving. And I enter into Your courts with praise. I praise You because You are worthy. You are holy. You are righteous and just.

I declare that the spirit of excellence rests upon me. And that my realm is engaged in my assignments. I call it charged with the names of God. Jehovah Jireh, Jehovah Rapha. Jehovah Shammah, Jehovah Nissi, Jehovah Tsidkenu, Jehovah Mekadesh, Jehovah Ra'ah, Jehovah Shalom, Jehovah Gibbor, Jehovah Elohim, Jehovah Sabaoth. Jehovah Izzuz, Jehovah Hoseenu, El Shaddai, El Elyon, El Olam, El Roi, Yeshua Hamashiach.

I cause my realm and life to come into interface with the Seven Spirits of God. The Spirit of the

Lord, The Spirit of Wisdom and Understanding, The Spirit of Counsel and Might, The Spirit of Knowledge and the Fear of the Lord.

I plead the Blood of Jesus over myself, my dwelling place, my spouse, my children, my cars, my bank account, in everything under my stewardship.

Father, I pray that Your Heavenly Host, Your Angels, would guard this dwelling place roundabout both above and below and against every dimensional access point, in Jesus' Name.

I will say of the Lord that You are my refuge and my fortress, my God; in You will I trust.

I thank You, Lord, that, You set a hedge of Fire about me and no plague will come near my dwelling.

I now bring the authority of the Lord Jesus Christ and the fullness of the work of Christ, His Cross, resurrection, and ascension against every foul power, witchcraft, and black art. I cut them off, in the Name of the Lord.

No weapon formed against me shall prosper.

I bring the Cross and the Blood of Jesus Christ against every form of hex, vex, and incantation against every spell, ritual, vow, dedication, and sacrifice. Against every word, judgment, and curse from every evil altar. I command them broken and bound from my home, my family and myself this night, in the Name of the Lord Jesus Christ.

I now bring the authority of the Lord Jesus Christ and the fullness of the work of Christ between me and all people, their spirit, soul and body, their sin, warfare, and corruption.

Any evil pursuers, anyone who's attempting evil against me, my family, my home, my life, my business, my career, my ministry--. I send every human spirit bound back to their own body.

I command all of their sin, warfare and corruption bound back to the work of Christ in their life, and I forbid it to transfer to me.

Father, I thank You in advance that every curse, hex spell, incantation, voodoo, sorcery, form of witchcraft, dark art, or other forms of weaponized demonic activity sent against me is sent back to the pit of Hell from whence it came, to the evil *spirits* that sent it, sevenfold that they would know that Jesus is Lord.

Moreover, I pray that every human spirit, fallen angel, fallen angelic spirit, or otherwise malevolent *spirit* attempting to come against me or my household, would be apprehended by Your Heavenly Hosts such that they cannot even so much as set their foot upon this property.

Surround me with a wall of Fire, Lord God.

I pray that they would be escorted out to wherever the Lord Jesus sends them, pierced through with many arrows, and discomforted by Your lightning, in the process that they would know that Jesus is Lord.

Furthermore, I cancel and render powerless all attempts at mind-to-mind communication, dream manipulation, astral projection, and all other forms of psychic and telepathic intrusion, in the Name of Jesus.

I thank You that all my dreams are inspired by Your Holy Spirit. I declare that my sleep will be sweet, and uninterrupted. And that upon waking, I will be well rested.

I also put on the Armor of Light. I take up the Helmet of Salvation, the Breastplate of Righteousness, and the Belt of Truth. I declare that my feet are shod with the Preparation of the

Gospel of Peace, and I take up the Shield of Faith to quench all the fiery darts of the wicked one. And the Sword of the Spirit. Which is the Word of God.

I command the night.

I command the night to take hold of the ends of the Earth and shake the wicked out of it.

I will have dominion over the works of the devil in the morning. Lord, make the outgoings of the morning to rejoice.

I receive your loving kindness every morning.

Lord, release the beauty of Your holiness from the womb of the morning.

I bind the screech owl, in the Name of Jesus.

I bind any attack upon my life at night, I take authority over every demon that is released against me and my family at night. Let the evening tide trouble the enemies that would attack my life, in the Name of Jesus.

I bind and rebuke every *spirit* that would come against me at night, I bind and rebuke the pestilence that walks about in darkness. I will res at night because I dwell in safety. And the Lord gives me sleep.

Lord, set Your angels to guard and protect me at night or give me the deliverance in the night. season. Lord, instruct me in the night season.

Your song will be with me in the night. I will meditate upon you in the night watches. I receive Your knowledge in the night.

I receive Your faithfulness every night.

I bind and rebuke every vampire *spirit,* in the Name of Jesus.

I bind and rebuke all incubus, succubus, and evil marine *spirits* that would attack at night, in the dream or in the sleep, in the Name of Jesus.

I bind and take authority over all nightmares, night terrors, and demonic dreams, in the Name of Jesus.

Let the evening tide trouble the enemy that would attack my life, in the Name of Jesus.

I command the night to take hold of the ends of the Earth and shake the wicked out of it.

O Lord, let Your light break forth in my life as the morning. Let Your judgments come up on the enemy morning by morning. Lord, Your going forth is prepared as the morning.

We pray that You will come as the rain as the latter and the former rain upon the Earth.

Lord, You visit me every morning, and You awaken me morning by morning, and I thank You. You wake me in my ear to hear.

I will not be afraid of the arrow that flies by day, nor the terror that comes at night.

Lord, show forth Your salvation in my life from day-to-day.

I seal these declarations across every realm, every age, every timeline, and dimension, past, present, and future, to infinity.

I am blessed lying down and also when I rise.

I am also blessed, fruitful and prosperous, in the mighty Name of Jesus.

Amen.

Other books by this author

(Related books are pictured with links.)

AK: The Adventures of the Agape Kid

AMONG SOME THIEVES

Ancestral Powers https://a.co/d/9gPaa9A

Astral Projecting Spirit Spouse, DIE!

Barrenness, *Prayers Against*
https://a.co/d/feUltIs

Battlefield of Marriage, *The*

Beauty Curses, *Warfare Prayers Against*

https://a.co/d/6pJulpZ

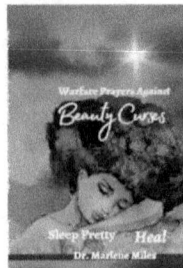

Behave

Blindsided: *Has the Old Man Bewitched You?*
This book gives more of the background of
the astral projecting wizard in the book:
Astral Projecting Spirit Spouse, DIE!

https://a.co/d/5O2fLLR

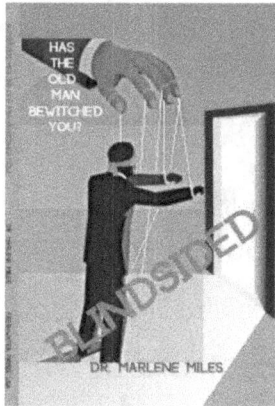

Break Free From Collective Captivity

Churchzilla, The Wanna-Be, Supposed-to-be
Bride of Christ

Courts of Marriage: Prayers for Marriage in
the Courts of Heaven (prayerbook)

Courtroom Warfare @ Midnight
(prayerbook)

Curses of Blind Men

Demonic Cobwebs (prayerbook)
https://a.co/d/7prRy1e

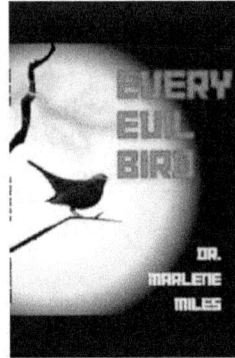

Demonic Time Bombs

Demons Hate Questions

Devil Loves Trauma, *The*

Devil Weapons: Unforgiveness, Bitterness,…

The Devourers: Thieves of Darkness 2

Do Not Swear by the Moon

Don't Refuse Me, Lord (4 book series)
https://a.co/d/idP34LG

Dream Defilement https://a.co/d/dJLjb3c

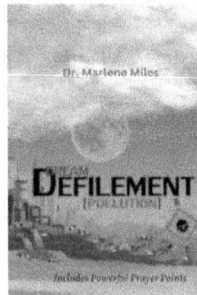

The Emptiers: *Thieves of Darkness, 1*

Every Evil Bird https://a.co/d/ibaETXw

Evil Touch https://a.co/d/eyBHqko

Failed Assignment https://a.co/d/cPOG3Z4

Fantasy Spirit Spouse
https://a.co/d/8YfRxmq

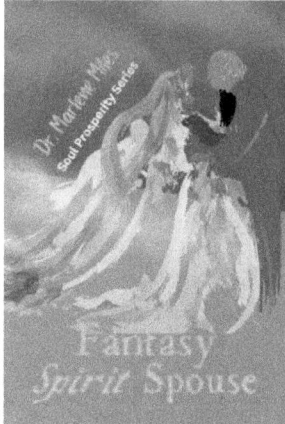

FAT Demons (The): *Breaking Demonic Curses*

The Fold (5 book series)

The Fold (Book 1)

Name Your Seed (Book 2)

The Poor Attitudes of Money (3)

Do Not Orphan Your Seed (4)

For the Sake of the Gospel (5)

Fruit of the Womb:

Gates of Thanksgiving

Gathered

got HEALING? Verses for Life

got LOVE? Verses for Life

got HOPE? Verses for Life

got money? https://a.co/d/g2av41N

How to Dental Assist

How to Dental Assit2: Be Productive, Not Wasteful

I Take It Back https://a.co/d/cHX40BJ
https://a.co/d/cHX40BJ

Legacy

Let Me Have A Dollar's Worth
https://a.co/d/h8F8XgE

Level the Playing Field

Living for the NOW of God

Lose My Location https://a.co/d/crD6mV9

Man Safari, *The*

Marriage Ed. Rules of Engagement &
Marriage

Made Perfect in Love

Money Hunters: Beware of Those

Money on the Altar

Mulberry Tree, *The (forthcoming)*

Motherboard (The) - soul prosperity series

Name Your Seed

Occupy: *Until I Return*

Plantation Souls

Players Gonna Play

Power Money: Nine Times the Tithe

The Power of Wealth *(forthcoming)*

Powers Above

The Robe, Part 1, The Lessons of Joseph

The Robe, Part II, The Lessons of Joseph

Seasons of Grief

Seasons of Waiting

Seasons of War

Second Marriage, Third--, Any Marriage

Sift You Like Wheat

Spirits of Death, Hell & the Grave, Pass Over Me and My House

Soul Prosperity soul prosperity series 3

https://a.co/d/5p8YvCN

Souls Captivity soul prosperity series 2

The Spirit of Poverty

StarStruck

SUNBLOCK

The Swallowers: *Thieves of Darkness*, 3

This Is NOT That: How to Keep Demons from Coming at You

Throne of Grace: Courtroom Prayer

Time Is of the Essence

Too Many Wives: *Why You Have Lady Problems*

Tormenting Spirits   https://a.co/d/dAogEJf

Toxic Souls

Triangular Power *(series)*
https://a.co/d/a8R4Rd7

Uncontested Doom

Unguarded Hours, *The*

Unseen Life, *The* (forthcoming)

Upgrade: How to Get Out of Survival Mode

      Toxic Souls (Book 2 of series)

      Legacy (Book 3 of series)

Warfare Prayer Against Beauty Curses

Warfare Prayer Against Poverty

Wasted, Don't be Defeated by the Waster Spirit: *Thieves of Darkness,* Book 2 (forthcoming)

What Have You to Declare? What Do You Have With You from Where You've Been?

When I Was A Child, I Prayed As a Child

When the Devourer is Rebuked

The Wilderness Romance *(series)*

- *The Social Wilderness*
- *The Sexual Wilderness*
- *The Spiritual Wilderness*

Credits:

Prayer Against Human Persecutors, Prayers That Shake Heaven and Earth, Dr. Daniel Duval https://a.co/d/6Wal9ru

Some prayer points adapted from Dr. Anthony O. Akerele, Evil Spiritual Marriage: Everyone Has A Spirit Spouse https://a.co/d/aClGQ2c

Command the Night prayer is a compilation by Dr. Daniel Duvall and Wild at Heart Ministries. https://wildatheart.org/

Prayed on Warfare Prayer Channel by this author: https://www.youtube.com/watch?v=ZldpAtiBt2s